ANGER MANAGEMENT

7 Steps to Freedom from Anger, Stress, and Anxiety

© **Copyright 2017 by Ryan James - All rights reserved.**

The following Book is reproduced below with the goal of providing information that is as accurate and as reliable as possible. Regardless, purchasing this Book can be seen as consent to the fact that both the publisher and the author of this book are in no way experts on the topics discussed within, and that any recommendations or suggestions made herein are for entertainment purposes only. Professionals should be consulted as needed before undertaking any of the action endorsed herein.

This declaration is deemed fair and valid by both the American Bar Association and the Committee of Publishers Association and is legally binding throughout the United States.

Furthermore, the transmission, duplication or reproduction of any of the following work, including precise information, will be considered an illegal act, irrespective whether it is done electronically or in print. The legality extends to creating a secondary or tertiary copy of the work or a recorded copy and is only allowed with express written consent of the Publisher. All additional rights are reserved.

The information in the following pages is broadly considered to be a truthful and accurate account of facts, and as such any inattention, use or misuse of the information in question by the reader will render any resulting actions solely under their purview. There are no scenarios in which the publisher or the original author of this work can be in any fashion deemed liable for any hardship or damages that may befall them after undertaking information described herein.

Additionally, the information found on the following pages is intended for informational purposes only and should thus be considered, universal. As befitting its nature, the information presented is without assurance regarding its continued validity or interim quality. Trademarks that mentioned are done without written consent and can in no way be considered an endorsement from the trademark holder.

Table of Contents

Introduction: The Anger Problem 1

Chapter 1: The Origins of Anger.. 7

Chapter 2: What is Anger good for?... 19

Chapter 3: Justified vs. Unjustified Anger.............................. 31

Chapter 4: Handling Different Types of Anger 41

Chapter 5: Long-lasting Anger 55

Chapter 6: Being Angry at Yourself...63

Chapter 7: Healthy Outlets for your Anger 69

Conclusion 89

Thank you!... 91

INTRODUCTION

THE ANGER PROBLEM

Congratulations on purchasing your personal copy of *Anger Management: 7 Steps to Freedom from Anger, Stress, and Anxiety*. Thank you for doing so.

Everyone knows how anger feels since we have all experienced it, whether just as a momentary annoyance or full-on rage-filled fury. Anger is normal and usually healthy for those who experience it. However, when this normal emotion is allowed to run rampant and turn destructive, it causes many issues with personal relationships, your career, and eventually poisons your entire life. In addition, anger can lead you to feel like you're being controlled by something powerful and unpredictable. This book is intended to help you both control and understand anger.

The Norm of Anger and Attack Tactics:

Perhaps it's a bit ironic that during this modern age of positive thinking and psychology, anger is one of the most commonly expressed emotions on a social level. Countless politicians have thrown in the towel on trying to give a dignified debate. Instead, they scream, yell, shove, and push at the slightest provocation. There was a time when attack advertisements were only reserved for very serious or bad situations, but this is now the most common tactic used in politics.

These attacks aren't only reserved for political views and even go into personal details about the politician's life. These attacks may occur in comments that are meant to be off the record or show up in voice recordings.

But this anger is not limited to just politics. It seems like a daily occurrence that we either read about or witness someone attacking a customer service agent, drivers and their road rage and outbursts of overworked professionals. There are plenty of theories about where this comes from, ranging from a lack of home stability, the state of the economy, teachers failing to instill politeness in their pupils, the Internet, the government, or even food chemicals.

Reasons behind the Anger Problem:

Brain and Psychology researchers discuss the amygdala (which controls our emotions in the brain) being too small or too large, or even underdeveloped pre-frontal cortexes in the brain (which are responsible for planning). Social studies look to the role of vicarious reinforcement and modeling for triggering this angry, aggressive behavior, while other psychologists blame this aggression on weak superegos. The bottom line is that there are theories everywhere, but the problem persists.

The following chapters will discuss some of the many ways you can better understand the issue of anger in yourself (and the anger of others), so you can fix the problem and stop letting this aggression run your life.

There are plenty of books on this subject on the market, thanks again for choosing this one! Every effort was made to ensure it is full of as much useful information as possible. Please enjoy!

Your Free Gift

As a way of saying thanks for your purchase, I wanted to offer you a free bonus E-book called *"How to Talk to Anyone: 50 Best Tips and Tricks to Build Instant Rapport"*.

Within this comprehensive guide, you will find information on:

- How to make a killer first impression
- Tips on becoming a great listener
- Using the FORM method for asking good questions
- Developing a great body language
- How to never run out of things to say
- Bonus chapters on Persuasion, Emotional Intelligence, and How to Analyze People

To grab your free bonus book just tap here, or go to:

http://ryanjames.successpublishing.club/freebonus/

CHAPTER 1

THE ORIGINS OF ANGER

Anger is a state of emotion that spans from light irritation to overwhelming rage and fury. Similar to other feelings, anger is accompanied by biological and physiological changes. As soon as you get angry, your blood pressure and heart rate increase along with the energy hormones noradrenaline and adrenaline. Anger is caused by internal and external events alike.

You might get angry at someone, like a supervisor or coworker, or a situation (such as a canceled flight or traffic jam), or you might get angry from brooding or worrying about personal issues in your life. In addition, remembering enraging or traumatic events can trigger this emotion. Where exactly does this problematic tendency come from? Understanding this will help you get your own anger and frustration under control so that you can lead a free and healthy life.

The Increasingly Angry World:

We gave some possible explanations for the norm of anger in the introduction to this book. Even professional psychologists who study anger don't have all the answers, but social factors play a large role. Apart from physical brain factors, the social order does seem to be coming unglued in a few different ways, including the polarization of the political spectrum, the shrinking economy, and reality TV. But there are some subtle, smaller ways that we are losing our composure.

Depictions of Anger on Television:

Anger is slowly becoming the norm. First instance, consider the way some television shows depict characters consulting professionals for advice on something, such as lawyers, nurses, or doctors. If someone on House, for instance, doesn't approve of his diagnosis, he will curse at his doctor. In everyday shows that many people watch, the characters speak to each other as though they are enemies, and this is considered normal.

The Role of Observing Aggression:

Observing this aggressive behavior, especially when it doesn't cause negative results, could be playing an important role in provoking aggressive outbursts in the average person. Human behavior studies involve a lot of factors that might compound upon each other, which explains why the area often uses nonhuman animals to get its results. One study done recently by Loyola University tested the idea that passive observation and brain chemistry can lead to higher aggressive actions in mice.

The mice who observed angry behavior in other mice developed a higher amount of neural receptivity in their brains than the mice who didn't. In other words, by just watching their rodent companions fight, the ones observing developed a higher tendency toward feeling aggression in themselves.

Childhood Aggression and Modeling:

Ironically, the increasingly violent cartoons of the '50s are what led psychologists to look into modeling's role in aggression in kids. The idea that the more kids watched violent shows, the more they showed violent tendencies, supported the conclusion that anger breeds anger.

This is one of the many reasons why the study about the mice above is so valuable. You might wonder, then, where the anger originally came from.

Presumably, anger and aggression have always existed in humans. A world free from violence will probably never exist, but the problem is determining its consequences. This behavior will never stop if no obvious consequences occur, escalating and eventually causing more harm.

Too much Violence and Rage?

If the consensus is that too much violence, rage, and aggression is being perpetuated in society and the media, what are we to do? The tide is probably too advanced to stop completely, but we can hope that manners will become popular again. In the meantime, it's up to the individual to notice when they are acting inappropriate and learn to control their own aggression. You can start by taking responsibility for the role you play yourself in this societal problem.

The Expression of Anger:

The natural, instinctive way to express a feeling of anger is to act in an aggressive way. Anger is an adaptive, natural reaction to a threat and inspires strong, usually aggressive behaviors and feelings in us. This allows us to defend ourselves and fight when we are under threat or attack. A certain level of this emotion, then, is needed for our species to survive.

But we cannot reasonably lash out physically every time someone or something annoys or irritates us. Common sense, social norms, laws, and our own sanity put limits onto how much we can express this emotion. Plus, it wouldn't be good for us to act on every impulse we have that comes from anger. Society could never have progressed if everyone did this. There's a reason we matured past this.

The Three Approaches to Anger:

Most individuals use a variety of unconscious and conscious methods for dealing with anger, which is calming, suppressing, and expressing. Let's look closer at each of these ways of dealing with it.

- **Expression:** Expressing anger in a way that is assertive instead of aggressive is the healthiest method of dealing with anger. In order to do this right, you must find out how to express your needs and meet them without harming other people. Assertiveness does not translate to being demanding or pushy with others, but being respectful both to others and yourself.

- **Suppression:** Alternatively, you can suppress anger, then redirect or convert it later on. This process occurs when you keep your anger inside, make yourself stop focusing on it, then redirect your mind to something more positive. The goal here is to suppress and inhibit the angry feeling, converting it to something more constructive and positive. The problem with this reaction is that if your anger isn't expressed outwardly, it can turn toward yourself. Inward anger may lead to depression, high blood pressure, hypertension, and other issues.

- Suppressing anger can lead to other issues for you, including pathological anger expressions, including passive aggression, or a hostile and cynical personality. Individuals who put other people down constantly, are always critical and make cynical comments are a perfect example of the consequences of not learning how to express anger constructively. People like this are, not surprisingly, not very likely to enjoy success with their relationships.

- **Calming Down**: The last method for dealing with anger is calming down inside. What this means is not only controlling the way you act outwardly, but controlling the responses you have inside, actively lowering your pulse, allowing the emotions to pass, and intentionally calming yourself.

The Anger Management Goal:

The main goal of learning about anger management should be reducing the physiological response and emotional feelings of anger. You can not avoid or get rid of the people or things that cause you to get mad, and you can't change most of them. Your reactions, however, are always within your control.

How can you Know if you're too Angry?

Now that you know the harm anger can cause, how are you to know if you need to work on your own anger? There are some tests out there that can gauge the intensity of this emotion, along with your abilities to handle it and how prone you are to anger. But the odds are high that if you have an anger issue, you're already well aware of it. After all, you're reading this book! If you notice that you act in frightening or out of control ways, you may need assistance in dealing with your anger.

What makes some Individuals Angrier than Other Individuals?

According to experts, certain people just have hotter heads than other people, getting mad faster and more intensely than is most common. There are also plenty of people who aren't as outwardly expressive with their angry feelings but who are always grumpy and irritable. People who are easily angered do not always throw things or curse, at times they just get ill, sulk, or withdraw socially.

People who get mad easily usually have what is known as a low frustration tolerance. In other words, they feel like they don't deserve to feel annoyance, inconvenience, or frustration in life. These people don't know how to take the events of life in stride and get especially mad when they encounter an "unfair" situation, such as being corrected.

The Causes of Easy Frustration:

What is that makes someone more prone to easy frustration? There are numerous factors at play here.

- **Genetics or Physiology:** One cause could be physiological properties or genetics. In fact, evidence exists that some kids are just born easily angered, touchy, or irritable and show these signals from a very young age.

- **Sociocultural Factors:** Another possible cause for getting easily angered is sociocultural factors. Anger is usually seen as something negative. Most of us are taught that we can show sadness or anxiety, but that anger is not tolerable. This can lead to an inability to channel the feeling in a constructive manner.

- **Family Background:** Studies have shown that family life also plays a big role in anger. Usually, those who get mad easily come from a background full of angry family members or a chaotic, disruptive home life. If a child is never taught how to deal with their anger, they likely won't be very good at communicating their emotions in a healthy way.

Should you Openly Express your Anger?

Some believe and claim that letting your anger show is the best way to prevent the harmful impacts of suppressing or ignoring it. Is this a good idea?

Professional psychologists are now stating that this is not a good idea. Some individuals will use the theory above as an excuse to be hurtful to those around them. Studies have shown that just letting your anger flow uninhibited actually causes aggression to escalate and doesn't help you fix the situation at all. The best approach is to figure out what is causing your anger and then to come up with methods for keeping these triggers in check instead of letting them send you flying off the handle.

CHAPTER 2

WHAT IS ANGER GOOD FOR?

Emotions are there for a reason, but anger can often seem pointless, confusing, or even harmful. Anytime you aren't getting what you wish for, or you get something you fear; it may cause anger to appear. Be careful, because excessive anger can cause divorce, damage your children, and harm your relationships at work and home. How effective are you at controlling your anger? In order to help prevent this from becoming a problem, learn to see this emotion as a sign that you should pause.

Anger, The Chemical Response:

Anger is triggered in reaction to chemicals from your primitive lower and middle brain areas. These chemicals are meant to mobilize us for defensive action to prevent harm. These chemicals are sending the message "GO!" to our body, spurring the animal to get what it needs to survive, by force if necessary. This helped us evolve by getting food first, dominating an enemy, or scaring off predators. It mobilizes your body for action to achieve important goals.

Anger to Self Soothe Neuro-chemically:

With some exceptions that are few and far between, most angry people have a problem with their self-image or self-esteem. A lot of them have success with their jobs but have a hard time with relationships, where there are plenty of anger triggers. Apart from their professional success, though, nearly all of these people have thoughts that they aren't good enough.

There is actually a chemical explanation for how the emotion of anger (at least temporarily) can be a type of soothing mechanism psychologically. The brain releases a hormone called norepinephrine when anger is sparked, which the brain experiences as an analgesic.

The Numbing Effect:

Whether someone is confronted with psychological or physical pain (or even the fear of pain like this), the response of anger helps to release chemicals to numb it. So anger is not a pointless emotion and exists for a reason. Anger can harm relationships, sure, but it's also important for helping vulnerable individuals survive relationships and life, in general.

Covering Core Pain:

This kind of anger is there to mask the core pains we all have. The key, stressful feelings that are within these core pains are feeling unloved, powerless, rejected, guilty, accused, unimportant, or ignored. All of these build an identity that is based on shame. It's only reasonable, then, that if eliciting anger in yourself can help to mask these unbearable or hurtful feelings, a person could eventually grow dependent on these feelings until they are addicted to them.

The idea of soothing oneself is very relevant in this regard. Everyone has to find ways to reassure or comfort themselves when his or her sense of identity is under threat, rather through dismissal, criticism, or some other outside event that leads the to feel invalidated or doubt themselves. If someone is healthy on a psychological level, he or she can use his or her inner resources to validate themselves, to admit that he or she might have made a mistake without suffering intolerable shame or guilt. However, if they don't feel good about themselves deep down, their sense of self will be unable to withstand these threats.

Anger as the Remedy:

What is the remedy for this situation? Even though it seems paradoxical, anger can be a way to soothe yourself, even though the emotion can destroy wellbeing and peace of mind. This is because our anger can invalidate whatever or whoever caused us to suffer a feeling of invalidation. If we adamantly deny the threat outside of us, we can claim that our own point of view is superior, restoring our mental and emotional security. Although our state of mind is not in harmony, and we might actually feel bad inside, our anger is still a defense that lets us feel more comfortable than we did before.

Invalidating Others:

This helps us think that we are not the ones that are inconsiderate, selfish, bad, or in the wrong. It must be our co-worker, neighbor, our child, or our partner.

True, our desperate response might be a way to self-soothe as the last possible resort, but it does work as a self-soothing mechanism, nonetheless. Simply put, if you cannot offer yourself comfort through validating yourself, this will be done by the invalidation of other people. And those who have severe depression usually haven't figured out how to get rid of this powerful but self-destructive defense mechanism.

Anger for Self-Empowerment:

Since anger helps us to medicate ourselves against pain on a psychological level, it's also effective for warding off powerlessness or other doubtful feelings. Our brain releases the numbing feeling when we get provoked, but it also releases amphetamine-related hormones, which allow us to feel energized by adrenaline. This can seem adaptive and very tempting. If a situation or person leads us to feel powerless or defeated, we can reactively transform those uncomfortable emotions into righteous anger and feel in control again.

The Cost of Lacking Skills in Anger Management:

But when someone doesn't have skills for managing his or her anger, instead of exploding aggressively, their reactions are very likely to lead to serious problems. These outbursts might get them what they want at the moment, but it clashes with other important needs. People wish to be loved and liked. Although anger may get you what you want in the immediate moment, it will weaken your attractiveness in terms of family connections, friendships, and work situations. To put it simply, angry people are less liked than agreeable people.

Anger helps you Notice Problems:

As soon as anger has shown you that you need to pay attention, it's done its job. But the madder you get, the less likely you are to effectively solve the issue. This is because aggression decreases your thinking ability, your ability to notice new information, to form new perspectives, or to create a good solution. Similar to your laptop, overheating will freeze up your data-processing mechanisms, shutting you down. As soon as anger has shown you that you need to pause because there's a problem, the best course of action is to obey this instruction.

Remembering to Pause:

The trick to controlling your anger is to keep in mind that it's meant to remind you to pause what you're doing. Anger shows you that you need to pause, listen, and look at your surroundings. Stop proceeding with the situation, stop and remind yourself to first lower your feelings of rage and aggression. Do some deep breathing, distract your mind with something more positive, relax your muscles, count backwards from 100, do whatever works best for you to pause.

Change the Subject:

Changing the subject can aid you in pausing a heated conversation or interaction, pausing the anger effectively. You can make a pleasant comment that derails the path that you were on previously. If this doesn't work for calming down the anger inside you, simply excuse yourself. You can say that you need to step outside or get some water.

This is your chance to soothe yourself using methods such as reading something, slowing your breath, or looking at pictures of cute puppies online. As soon as you've returned to calmness, you may start planning out the method you'll use to handle whatever situation is troubling you. Think of this as a time-out you give to yourself, as a parent gives to their toddler in the throes of a temper tantrum.

Pay Attention:

The next step here is to pay attention to the situation, seeing it from a different point of view that helps you figure out what you truly need and want from it. Come up with a smarter way to communicate than just attacking your conversation partner with words until you achieve your goals. Keep in mind that you may use words in a constructive way to think about the situation, come up with a plan, and address your concerns. You can use your logical reasoning abilities, as a human, to plan out what you can do differently the next time around.

Be Careful:

Be careful and steer clear of the trap that is always present when considering a difficult, anger-inducing problem or situation. Remember that you should be focusing on yourself instead of the event or person you're mad at. Stay away from thoughts about how you want the situation or person to change to make you happy. Thinking about how the person made you mad or what they should do to make up for what they did will only feed your anger and frustration.

Focus on you:

You should focus on what you can do to fix what happened, and on how you can change to be better at handling problems in the future. Becoming empowered to make changes yourself instead of thinking about controlling the other person or the situation is one key way to calmly handle anger with poise.

This will also help you overcome the urge to handle difficult scenarios with anger and aggression. Remind yourself repeatedly, starting from when the anger first starts appearing within you, that your job is to find what you can do to change the situation, not to control others.

Practice Listening:

This part is perhaps the most challenging of all. At this stage, you need to ask the other about their concerns. Make yourself stay calm and refrain from reacting, as you listen to them and search for the common ground between you two. Listen to them to gain a true understanding of what they feel, rather than defensively responding or attacking their point of view, as you may wish to do at the moment. Actually, the madder you are, the harder it will be to truly listen to the other person.

This is because when anger is present, it makes you feel like your desires are sacred and that others' don't matter. Your wishes will appear gigantic, as the other person's wishes shrink down to nothing.

Be Fully Calm:

This is why you must make sure you've calmed yourself all the way when you first pause. This is essential for true listening and will allow you to rise to the challenge of understanding the concerns of the other person. Thankfully, if you do truly listen fully enough to understand their perspective, you're going to have better odds of reaching your own goals, too. Even if this sounds paradoxical, it's the truth, as all skilled salespeople already know. The more in tune a salesperson is when their client's concerns, the better chance they have at reaching the agreement they want in the end. Remember that in order to reliably control your anger, when you get mad, pause.

Relationships, Health, and Self-Esteem:

The majority of people know that there's a connection between persistent anger and physical issues, such as heart disease. But anger also has other more obvious, immediate effects on the sufferer. It uses up a lot of physical and mental energy, steals your enjoyment of life, gets in the way of useful and constructive thinking, and harms your career and relationship prospects. Anger can also hurt your self-esteem and cause you to obsess over the negative thoughts circling in your mind.

Anger Victimizes you:

Once you have an aggressive exchange, you will suffer the effects for a while after, as you repeat what happened over and over in your head, bringing up the angry emotions again and adding power to them repeatedly. During this time, your emotions will be controlled by these angry memories, causing you to be victimized by your feelings.

Anytime you let someone's actions cause you anger, you're being victimized by your feelings. That person has probably already forgotten about the event while you are controlled by it. As you fret and fume and go over the event repeatedly, you are missing out on spending time with your family, relaxing on your day off, or while trying to fall asleep in your bed at home. As you can see, learning how to get this under control is very important for a happy, fulfilled life.

CHAPTER 3

JUSTIFIED VS. UNJUSTIFIED ANGER

Plenty of Americans go around feeling angry these days, and some have more justified reasons for this than others. Let's look at the differences between unjustified and justified anger.

Justified Anger:

People who are justified in their anger are the homeless, the unemployed, those who are hungry or who are taking on unmanageable tax burdens. Someone who cannot afford an education has justified anger or those who don't have enough health care. Those who have lost loved ones to war or who don't feel as though they have a choice in political situations all have justified anger, as well.

Unjustified Anger:

The people who have unjustified anger include people who don't take responsibility for their own actions, who blame others, or who feel as though they are always being victimized by life circumstances. It's the ones who always put their own needs first and don't think about others.

Does Anger give you the Illusion of Control?

If anger makes you feel as though you're actually in control, you will have a hard time controlling your anger. This heading sums up a lot of people's problem with anger. For those who are interested in this emotion, it can be hard to find clinical literature on it. But this is starting to change. With drive-by shootings, road rage, and high school killing sprees on the rise, people are starting to play closer attention to acting out, extreme anger, and acts of aggression.

Suddenly, paying attention to warning signs of anger seems a lot more important. Within the last 15 years, at least 50 books have emerged on the subject of anger. In the year 1995, a professional book called *Anger Disorders: Definition, Diagnosis, and Treatment* came out that proposed some diagnostic categories to handle anger as a syndrome, instead of a feeling connected to different disorders.

The following will be an attempt to make sense of the anger-related, self-defeating actions that arise from this emotion.

The Forgotten Defense:

Anger can be thought of as the forgotten defense of Freud. If, in Freud's opinion, every defense mechanism of the human mind is there to protect our personalities from the anxiety that comes from the ego being attacked, it's weird that he didn't consider anger as part of this.

Anger as Camouflage:

But when it comes to an essential human feeling that is mainly there to protect someone from another feeling, anger might be the exception. Anger almost never exists as the main, primary emotion. Even when it appears to be a knee-jerk, instantaneous response to being provoked, there is usually another feeling that was their fist. This primary feeling is what your anger is popping up to control or attempt to camouflage.

The Road Rage Example:

A simple example of this idea of anger would be the extremely frustrating experience of someone cutting you off in traffic. Nearly everyone that experiences this event reacts with anger. However, when you look deeper at what getting cut off in traffic usually involves, the danger of getting into a life-threatening accident, they notice that at the moment before taking action to avoid the crash, they felt some kind of fear or apprehension.

Switching from this level of apprehension or fear to the intense state of anger occurs so quickly that most people can't recall the flash of fear they had felt the anger or rage took over their mind. Even rage itself appears to be a more desperate, stronger type of anger that was created in mind to get rid of the threat to one's personal safety or ego, whether this is physical, emotional, or mental.

Secondary Anger and What It Means:

The inner process happening in the above example also applies to other emotions that, one they appear, can be hidden through a flash of secondary anger.

And as many psychological defenses get in the way of healthy coping mechanisms (by hiding the initial anxiety that must be faced), anger also shows how fragile the ego is that needs to be supported and shielded.

How Anger Controls us:

If anger leads us to a feeling of power and appears to be a magical solution to mask our deep fears and doubts, it's no wonder that it controls us in so many ways. In a way, anger is similar to cocaine or anger, causing strong addictions due to its illusory effect of empowering us. Though nearly no one realizes that their tendency toward getting angry is a way to cope with, intimidate, and disarm their enemy, anger is used as a way to make up for lack of self-esteem and personal power.

Unlike feeling out of control or weak, the emotion of aggression or anger causes a sensation of invincibility or invulnerability. In fact, anger can even have physical effects on someone, making them momentarily stronger with adrenaline.

Anger for Distancing in Relationships:

Anger also has a function in regulating the distance between us and others in close relationships, ensuring safety from getting hurt. If someone's parents or caretakers were untrustworthy, unreliable, or unresponsive, that person would probably grow up to be wary or defensive. They will likely cultivate a way to be emotionally detached in close relationships. Although these people might wish to form a strong bond that they've missed from childhood, they won't know how to express these desires and needs in an open, healthy way. Risking this with someone who may react in a negative way could hurt them gravely.

The Fear of Letting down your Guard:

The deep fear in these people is that letting their defense down and allowing themselves to be vulnerable, revealing their deep desire, could lead to rejection. A negative response could be very harmful to them, so they use anger as a protective measure and distance themselves as a way to survive emotionally.

Many spouses say that as soon as they notice their marriage going very well, their partner would pick a fight, probably due to feeling threatened by this closeness. Wounded psychologically from parental disregard, insensitivity, or even worse, they might have a serious distrust of getting too close to someone, defaulting to defensive anger as a way to protect themselves.

Using Anger to Push Someone Away:

On the other hand, anger can also push the other away from us, leading them to be the one to back off. If someone wants to get plenty of space and alone time, all he or she has to do is be angry all the time. This will cause others to avoid you at all costs. If we have no experience with relational intimacy, the feeling of being close to someone else can feel dangerous to our inner equilibrium, setting off alarms and causing anger. In this sense, the anger can be said to be justified, but still not healthy.

Too much Detachment:

But feeling very detached from others may also dredge up old fears and wounds, so sometimes, the one who wanted distance might pursue the other. The point to take from this is that even unconscious anger can be used in many ways that regulate the feeling of vulnerability when it comes to close relationships. This can not only be utilized to create distance with the other person when closeness causes anxiety, but can also be used as a way to try to engage the other person from a distance.

If we had an insecure or tenuous attachment to our parents growing up, it's logical that the least risky way to get attached to someone else would be using anger to create distance. Scared of being too close to someone else, but scared of completely breaking our attachment to them, getting angry easily presents a solution, even though it's unsatisfying and dysfunctional. You can ask yourself the following questions to have a better understanding of your anger:

- What skills should I learn for controlling my anger?

- What is my anger protecting me against?

- How can I address the core feeling behind my anger?

Anger can be compared to an emotion that is just the top of the iceberg. It's rarely there on its own and instead exists to hide other, deeper emotions happening below it.

CHAPTER 4

HANDLING DIFFERENT TYPES OF ANGER

When something occurs that brings your anger up without warning, it can be hard not to yield to this feeling. Since you will usually get mad from feeling fearful or powerless in response to an unfair event, anger appears as your attempt to bring a fast fix to the situation. This can be compared to steeling your body against an impending attack, but it all happens on a mental level, instead of physically.

But there are many different issues that come up when you give into this push-back response of feeling angry, and the main issue is likely that the anger almost never resolves the problem that caused it to arise. This reactive feeling of anger can be best understood as a self-destructive tendency. So how can you tell how to handle your anger?

Healthy, Logical Responses to Anger:

For anger to be acted on in a healthy way, it has to fit into two different criteria, which is nearly impossible in every case. For your anger reaction to make sense, it must:

1. Be in response to someone who has needlessly and intentionally acted in a way that was hurtful to you, and...

2. Be advantageous or beneficial for you (as in it must help you achieve the goal you have in your mind.

I think most people will see that you can almost never claim that anger is helpful and warranted, either to you or to the situation you're dealing with at the moment. So here is an alternative to giving into anger and abandoning all reason and logic. This should neutralize your feelings of anger within just seconds, or if you're in a serious rage, in a few minutes.

How to Neutralize Rage or Anger:

Remember that, for this to work, you have to actually wish to follow these steps, have enough motivation to go through with them, and overcome the subconscious resistance that's standing in your way. Since there are some immediate benefits that come along with anger that get in the way of your determination to defeat the anger, we will go over a few advantages that could get in the way of using this method to neutralize your harmful, self-destructive feelings of anger. Here is what anger accomplishes, at least at the moment:

- **Gives you a Reward:** Anger can make you feel as though you're morally superior in the situation. That justified feeling of righteousness works temporarily to bolster a weak sense of self-esteem and is used as a defense mechanism.

- **Defends against Fear:** Anger can defend against anxiety or vulnerability. When you get that righteous rush of anger, accompanied by adrenaline, it makes you feel momentarily empowered, which is better than afraid.

- **Protects against Depression:** Anger can help you avoid feeling depression, alienation, or a deep loneliness. Even though the interaction is likely negative, anger allows you to engage with someone else.

- **(Appears to) Restore Control:** Anger can help you regain a sense of control when you get frustrated and feel as though you have none. It can temporarily put the power back into your hands, or so it seems.

- **Helps you Get what you want:** Anger can aid you in getting what you want using intimidation tactics with the other person.

The Double Step Anger Control Technique:

If you have a hard time putting the process we are going to cover below into practice, these immediate benefits to anger are likely what is causing you to have trouble. You must first realize these advantages if you are going to work through them and learn to control your anger.

Step Number 1: Relaxation.

Your first step requires that you relax. Even though anger has made you feel as though your whole body is ready to fight (inspired by adrenaline and fear), you need to find a method for discharging that energy before moving onto any action whatsoever. You must realize that in order to go into battle mode, you are activating every organ and muscle in your body automatically.

Defined in a broad way, anger is basically the reaction to a threat that you perceived, so it serves as your body's signal to get ready for combat. Since your body is mobilized for impulsive and immediate action, any reflectiveness that you use to stall would handicap this. Anger impacts your thinking as strongly as it does your physical body.

When Anger Isn't Needed:

Considering the ethnical and legal limitations of living in modern society, it's not very likely that when you get angry, you will assault your spouse or even need to defend yourself physically. But anger gets your mind ready to fight, in addition to your body, so as soon as this emotion comes over you, you've already lost your ability to assess the event objectively or logically. This makes it likely that you will attack the person verbally.

At this stage, you are not thinking from a rational, evolved point of view, but the survival-oriented, primitive, and simple brain. This simple brain can be compared to a regressed, childlike state of mind where all you can focus on is being violated, cheated, devalued, disrespected, or disregarded. You then self-righteously crave to get revenge for this wrongdoing, immediately. It's like you believe that you can only bring the other person to justice by attacking them.

Regaining Emotional Equilibrium:

Since your thinking has been distorted or exaggerated by the anger, if you have any hope of regaining your emotional equilibrium, you must re-evaluate what happened from an adult point of view. This will need to happen before you can calm yourself. That's why the first thing you must do is calm yourself down, then you can move onto the second part of the process of getting your mind calm.

Find your Relaxation:

Hopefully, you already know how to calm yourself down when needed, whether it's deep breathing, meditation, music, guided imagery or visualization, yoga, acupressure, self-hypnosis, or another technique that works for you. However, if you haven't yet, you need to learn one first and foremost. Here are some ideas for doing that:

- **Research Breathing Exercises:** You could start by researching breathing exercises online, going with the one that seems most relevant to your situation. Stick with practicing this every day until you can pull it out and use it anytime you need to calm down.

- **Visualization:** For those who are more visually oriented, visualization can help a lot for relaxation. Imagine that you're on your favorite beach, taking a walk through a park, lying back on a floating cloud, next to a calm lake, or some other natural scene that feels relaxed to you. After you see the image in your mind, make sure you feel it in your body completely, reacting to these visual cues. Immersion is key here for effectiveness.

- If you are picturing being at the beach, for example, fantasize about smelling the air, seeing the landscape, hearing the waves against the shore, and feeling the sun on your face. The more of your senses you engage at this stage, the more success you will have. Your body cannot sense the difference between a well-imagined scenario and a true experience.

Remember, however, that no matter what technique you use to calm yourself down and reduce your physical arousal levels, even if it's just deep breathing, will work for this. The most important consideration is that instead of ventilating your anger, you pause and soothe yourself. You will find that this reduces your anger significantly.

And in the case that you still cannot relax yourself using these techniques, instead, try some exercise. Vigorous physical activity can be a method for releasing the tension in your body from your angry mood. These actions will allow your body to calm down, along with your mind, so that you can again think in a clear manner and find a solution. That brings us to the second step in this process.

Step Number 2: Re-Consider.

The second step is to re-assess and re-consider your situation, meaning find a way to see the situation from a positive, different point of view. Anger comes primarily from a negative attitude about what occurred. Change this outlook and your feelings around it will also change. You can ask yourself some of the following questions to do this:

- Did they actually mean what I thought they meant? Perhaps I am making assumptions about something before verifying the facts.

- Is this event as bad as I am making it out to be, or could I be exaggerating the situation and taking it too hard?

- Is the belief I have that this person is unjust a reflection of my own bias, rather than proof that they are unfair? Are their concerns and interests equally important as mine are?

- Is there a way I can shift my focus to something more positive instead of just thinking about what I dislike about the situation?

- What evidence is there that this person wanted to humiliate, hurt, or antagonize me intentionally? Do I need to take this so personally?

- Is there a way to view this person's objectives with more empathy instead of making them into the enemy?

- Did this person have a rational reason to say what they did? Maybe I can learn from what they have said to me instead of getting so angry.

- Is there a chance that they misunderstood me? Perhaps I wasn't as clear as I could have been and that's why they had such a negative reaction to what happened.

- Was that person joking, by chance? Perhaps my insecurities are what is making me feel so upset and angry.

- If they are truly nasty, mean, and inconsiderate to me, is there a situation where I have also done this to someone else?

There are likely 100 or more questions you could ask yourself any time you are feeling angry and vulnerable. Hopefully, these examples are enough to get the point across. Your anger didn't come from what happened, but the interpretation, negative meaning, or perception that you placed upon it. So you must come up with different ways to view what it was that angered you. Nearly every time, you will notice that a more measured, level-headed assessment of the event that caused this angry reaction will help to dissolve it.

Methods for being Gentler and less Angry:

When you have less anger on a daily basis, you will feel happier and more relaxed. Keep in mind that what happens in your life is only external and that you are the one who chooses to respond that way to them internally. Remind yourself consistently that no one else can force you to be mad and that ultimately, this intense emotion was created in your head, nowhere else. Here are some methods for keeping your anger under control, instead of allowing it to blaze out of control and cause problems:

- **Smile:** Any time you get angry because of a stranger, try smiling at them instead. This will disarm the person, who won't expect that reaction, but intentionally pausing the anger in its tracks can give you some much-needed perspective.

- **Count to 10:** There's a reason why this is age old wisdom that we all know about. Next time you feel angry, stop and count to 10, breathing deeply so you can regain a rational sense of mind.

- **Understand the Source:** Are you the type that gets angry easily with hardly any instigation? Maybe someone caused you pain as a child and now easily fall into the belief that you are being victimized, even when you aren't. Understanding where this tendency to get angry fast came from can help you rise above the emotion when it strikes.

- **Don't Pay Attention to Aggression:** When you feel tempted to add to the spread of anger over the Internet, resist it. The first step is noticing when you want to feed the fire, then resisting that impulse.

- **Notice other Perspectives:** When a person annoys you because they are delivering bad news, don't automatically believe that they are intentionally causing you pain. Most customer service workers aren't trying to personally wrong you. Think about being in their shoes before you react in anger.

Perhaps by learning to control your own anger, you can make the world a better place and inspire calmer, happier actions in others.

CHAPTER 5

LONG-LASTING ANGER

If you think that your anger problem is spiraling out of control, it's ruining your job or relationships, you may think about doing some counseling to find better ways to handle it. A licensed mental health practitioner can help you come up with methods for changing your actions and the thinking behind your anger.

Before choosing a counselor, you will likely meet with a few prospects. When you do, let them know that you have an anger problem that needs some work, or finds out about their anger management methods. There's nothing wrong with getting professional help, and for some anger issues, this may be the only way to truly heal.

Minimizing the Effects of Anger:

Sure, therapy isn't the only way to develop better methods for dealing with anger, but it can help you get in touch with your emotions and find better ways to show them. A lot of people who struggle with anger have this problem. Therapy can help you move to a more neutral anger range within two to three months, depending on the methods and circumstances.

Anger Management and Assertiveness Training:

Angry people must first learn assertiveness (as opposed to aggression), but the majority of courses and books about becoming more assertive are marketed for those who aren't in touch with their anger. The ones these books are written tend to be more on the passive side of things than is most common, allowing people to take advantage of them. This is not what someone who struggles with an anger problem does. But books such as these can still contain some useful information for controlling your frustration and being more assertive and constructive in conversation.

Remember, you can never completely get rid of anger, and even if you could, it wouldn't be smart or healthy. Regardless of how much you try to change the fact, events will always occur in life that leads you to feel angry, and at times, you will be justified in that anger.

Changing your Reactions and Attitudes:

Life will always come with loss, pain, frustration, and annoyance caused by what others do. You can never change this, but you can alter the way you react to these events and people. Getting your anger under control now will give you more lasting happiness in the future.

The Habit of Logic

If you can get into the habit of using logic when you get angry, you can defeat your anger. When anger occurs, even unjustified, it can easily spiral into the irrational. So if you use rational logic to defuse it, telling yourself that the world isn't against you, you're just having a hard day, it will become much easier. This can be done every time you feel your anger threatening to take over and beat you, and it will bring you a point of view that is much more balanced.

Becoming aware of your Demanding Ways:

People who get angry often usually demand what they want, whether it's willingness from others, agreement on their ideas, appreciation, or general fairness. All humans wish for these things and get disappointed and hurt when they don't work out. However, angry people demand these things and get disappointed, then mad when others don't meet their demands.

Prefer, don't Demand:

As a way to restructure your habits, you can begin becoming aware of this tendency in yourself and start using words such as "I would prefer" or "I'd like this" instead of demanding things to be a certain way. When you don't get what you wish for, you'll likely become disappointed, frustrated, and hurt, but anger won't be as common for you. A lot of angry people believe that if they jump to being mad, they are avoiding their pain, but the pain doesn't go away, it's just hidden under another layer and being expressed in another way.

Learning better Communication Habits:

People who get angry a lot often jump to conclusions, then act on them without thinking much into it. The problem is that their conclusions are often false, especially when jumped to in the heat of the moment. What you should do next time you are having a heated discussion is a pause, and give some thought to how you will respond.

- **Careful Consideration:** Saying the first thing you want to say when you get mad is a recipe for disaster. Instead, carefully consider what you want to communicate and the best way to do this.

- **Listen Carefully:** As you consider your responses, make sure you are also listening closely to the person you're speaking with. Try to also listen to what lies beneath the anger. For example, maybe you want some space while your partner is seeking to be closer. If they begin complaining about how you're acting, resist the urge to tell them they are clingy or wrong for feeling the way they do.

- **Pay Attention to the Defensive Signal:** Defensiveness is a quick way to get into a fight with someone else, and it's only natural to feel defensive if you are getting criticized, but resist the urge to fight back. Rather, pay attention to what is underneath the words being spoken. Perhaps your partner is feeling unloved and neglected. You may need some time to calm down before discussing, but don't allow your anger to make the talk spiral into a bad place. Staying calm is the difference between a huge fight and a constructive discussion.

Restructuring your Brain:

To put this simply, it involves changing your thinking habits. People who are angry usually swear, curse, or speak in intense, negative terms that express their feelings and thoughts.

- **Replacing Dramatic Phrases:** When you're mad, your ways of thinking tend to be overly dramatic and ridiculously exaggerated. You can stall the storm by replacing these dramatic thoughts with more reasonable ideas. For example, rather than saying to yourself "This day is ruined, everything is awful," say "This is frustrating, and it's reasonable to get upset, but being angry won't solve anything."

- **Avoid Absolutes:** Part of dramatic, negative thinking relies on using absolute statements. Pay attention to your thoughts and words and make sure you don't use the words "always" or "never." Using statements like these only make you feel as though your madness is fair and justified and that no solution exists. In addition, this can humiliate and alienate those you are speaking to and prevent agreements.

Most importantly, get into the habit of reminding yourself that being angry won't fix the problem and will make you less likely to find a workable solution for the problem.

Switching up your Environment:

At times, it's your surroundings that are causing you to feel angry and irritated. Responsibilities and problems can pile up on you until you feel like you're about to explode. Remember to give yourself some time to decompress every once in a while. Just 20 minutes of quiet time to yourself can make all the difference between staying calm and acting out of anger.

CHAPTER 6

BEING ANGRY AT YOURSELF

When you're angry at yourself, simple tools of relaxation, such as relaxing visualization and deep breathing, can help to calm you. Many angry people would believe that this is too simple to actually work, but they are selling themselves short, in that case.

Simple Relaxation Tools:

Oftentimes, we give ourselves excuses like that just to avoid making the changes that need to be made in ourselves. There are courses and other books that give effective techniques for relaxation, and learning them gives you a new toolset to use in all situations.

If you are married to or dating someone who is also hot-tempered, both of you would benefit from learning techniques such as these. Here are some techniques you can begin practicing today.

Breathing Techniques:

The first technique involves breathing deeply, from your belly instead of your chest. Trying to breathe deeply from the chest is not relaxing. Instead, picture it coming from deep inside of your abdomen.

Using a Mantra:

Use a repeated mantra to keep yourself calm, such as "take it easy" or "relax." As you breathe deeply, say this to yourself again and again until it becomes automatic.

Stretching:

Stretching can be a good way to diffuse tension and anger in yourself, relaxing your body and helping you feel a lot calmer. Stretching feels great and instantly helps you feel better.

Sticking to it:

Perhaps the most important technique of all is remaining dedicated to learning how to relax when you get angry. After a while, you will be able to call upon these techniques any time you start to feel frustrated.

Effective Problem-Solving:

At times, our frustration and anger are caused by inescapable, real issues that we are dealing with. Not all of our anger is unjustified and is often a natural, healthy way of reacting to difficult situations. We also have an expectation that for every problem, a solution exists, so we get extra frustrated when this isn't true, sometimes. The best way to deal with situations such as this, then, is not to think about the solution, but to think about your attitude in regards to the problem at hand.

- **Come up with a Plan:** Create a plan and check in on your progress as you go. Decide that you are going to try your best but don't punish yourself when things don't go exactly as you would prefer the to go.

- **Keeping Patience:** Remember that if you can approach problems with the best of efforts and intentions and give it your all, you will have a lot easier of a time staying patient, even in the face of difficulties. This way, you will stay logical, even when the issue doesn't go away immediately.

Using Silly Humor to Defuse Anger:

Humor can help you get rid of anger in a few different ways. Primarily, it can give you a perspective that is more logical and balanced.

Picturing bad Names:

When you're mad and want to call someone a bad name, like a dirtbag, instead, pause and think about the word literally. For instance, you would picture a huge bag of dirt sitting in front of you. Doing this can help you calm down instantly, and humor is always helpful for tense situations.

Using your Imagination:

The main message that an angry person tells themselves is that they should always get their way, that they are to the right, and that they should never have to be inconvenienced, even if other people do. Next time you feel these emotions, picture yourself like a king or queen, walking the streets and stores, always getting your way while other people have to answer to you. If you can be very detailed in this imagining, you will likely realize that you're not very reasonable and that what you're worried about isn't that important.

Be Careful with Humor:

If you do use humor to defuse your anger, you should be cautious. Don't attempt to use it to laugh off or ignore your problems, but instead to see them in a more constructive way. Also, don't mistake healthy humor for angry sarcasm, which is just another way of expressing unhealthy anger patterns.

Other Techniques for Going Easier on Yourself:

These techniques all have one thing in common; remembering not to take life, or yourself, so seriously. Anger does feel serious, sure, but the ideas behind it can seem funny from the right perspective.

- **Changing Timing:** If your spouse and you have a pattern of arguing when you talk in the evening, maybe this is due to being distracted, tired, or just having a bad habit. You can shake this up by changing what time of day you talk.

- **Avoid Stress Triggers:** If you feel stressed out each time, you see your daughter's messy room, close her door instead of making it a habit of focusing on what makes you angry. The point is not to justify your anger and keep it there but to learn how to become calmer.

- **Look for Alternatives:** Pay attention to what triggers your anger, such as commuting through heavy traffic on the way home from work. Then you can learn to plan around this and find alternatives, such as finding a better route.

The quickest way to make your anger worse is to feel guilty about it or beat yourself up. Remember to forgive yourself for feeling angry.

CHAPTER 7

HEALTHY OUTLETS FOR YOUR ANGER

Anger is a healthy, normal feeling, but it can be unhealthy when it gets out of control or flares up very often. Explosive, chronic anger will lead to serious problems for your health, relationships, and mental state. Thankfully, you can get your anger under control, and it may be easier than you thought. As soon as you figure out why you feel so angry and use the tools given to you in this book, you can keep your anger from taking over your everyday life.

Why should you Control but not Smother Anger?

Anger is neither bad nor good. Similar to our other feelings, anger is giving us a message, letting us know that something threatening, unjust, or upsetting is occurring. If you feel anger and have the reaction of wanting to explode, though, you have no chance to heed this message. So although it's normal to feel anger when something goes wrong, you're wronged, or someone mistreats you, anger is an issue when you are harming other people or yourself by expressing it.

Anger Facts and Myths:

If your temper is hot, you might think that you can't control it, but it's possible to learn healthier ways to express your feelings. You're in control, not your emotion.

The Myth: You shouldn't hold your anger in, it's better to vent it.

The Fact:

Although it's true that ignoring your anger isn't good for you, letting it out without discrimination isn't any better. Anger doesn't need to be let free in a forceful or aggressive way to prevent yourself from exploding. Actually, tirades and outbursts just add to the problem, reinforcing it.

The Myth: Intimidation, aggression, and anger will get you what you want.

The Fact:

You can't get others to truly respect you through bullying them. They might be afraid, but you cannot handle differing opinions if you have no control over your anger. Other people are far more likely to listen and work with you if you are more respectful in your communication.

The Myth: Anger is out of your control and cannot be changed.

The Fact:

You cannot control every situation you come into contact with, or even the way you feel about it, but you have control over the way you express these feelings. Anger can be expressed without physical or verbal abuse. Even when another person is really getting on your nerves, your response is always a choice.

Being Honest about your Anger:

You may believe that showing your anger every time it comes up is healthy, that other people are too thin-skinned, that you have every justification for being mad, or that you must show anger for others to take you seriously. But the fact of the matter is that this emotion will impair your better judgment, hurt those around you, and have an overall bad effect on your self-image and how others view you.

- **The Point of Managing Your Anger:** A lot of people believe that anger management relies on avoiding or suppressing angry feelings, but the goal is not to never feel mad. Anger is healthy and normal, as stated before, and will be expressed even if you try to avoid it. Your goal with learning how to manage is not to avoid or suppress it but to have a deeper understanding of what the feeling is trying to tell you, and find better ways to express it. This will help you feel better, meet your needs, manage confrontation and conflict, and have stronger, healthier relationships.

- **The Importance of Practice:** Managing anger is not the easiest thing you will ever do, but practice will make it much easier and the benefits are endless. When you learn how to both control and healthily express this feeling, you will be a lot likelier to reach the success you dream of.

The Dangers of Rampant Anger:

Anger that runs out of control is harmful to your physical body. Living with high-stress levels will leave you open to a higher chance of insomnia, a weak immune system, diabetes, heart and blood pressure issues. What else can it do?

- **Harm you Mentally:** Long-lasting anger will take up large amounts of your thought space and mental energy, clouding your reasoning abilities and making it much more difficult to enjoy life or even concentrate on anything. It will cause you depression, anxiety, and over harmful mental issues if not looked at.

- **Harm you Professionally:** Creative differences, constructive critique, and even heated arguments can lead to healthy results. However, lashing out in frustration will only alienate you from your clients, supervisors, and co-workers, making them think less of you and have a harder time being honest.

- **Harm your Relationships:** Anger causes scars that don't disappear in the people you love. When you explode in anger, other people will be far less likely to trust you, be honest with you, or even want to be around you.

Look Beneath the Emotion:

To reach healthy outlets for your anger, you must first look beneath the emotion itself. Anger issues usually come from things you learned in childhood. If you saw your parents yell, throw things, and argue all the time, you may believe that these are normal expressions of frustration or anger. High-stress levels and trauma as a kid can also leave you open to bad anger habits, as well.

- **Anger hides Other Emotions:** To learn how to express anger in healthy and appropriate ways, first, you have to get in touch with your true feelings. Are your outbursts there to mask other emotions like vulnerability, shame, hurt, insecurity, or embarrassment? If you have a common response to anger, you are probably using it to hide other emotions.

- **Looking to your Upbringing:** If you grew up in a situation where sharing emotion wasn't encouraged, this is even more likely. Now that you've grown up, you might have difficulty noticing any emotions apart from frustration or anger. In addition, anger can signal other health issues like chronic stress or trauma.

Is there more to this Emotion in you?

It can be hard to tell if your anger is just anger or if there's more beneath this emotion in you. Here are some signs that your anger is harboring more than it appears to be:

- **You can't Compromise:** Do you have difficulty understanding the perspectives of others or conceding your points of view? If you had an upbringing surrounded by out of control anger, you might be imitating patterns that you observed as a kid, believing that anger will get you what you want. The idea of compromise might make you feel vulnerable or like a failure.

- **You aren't in Touch with other Emotions:** Are you a tough person who is always in control of situations, no matter what? Do you think that feelings such as shame, guilt, or fear are not part of your life? Every person has those feelings, so if you think you don't, you're likely using aggression or anger to cover them up.

- **Opinions that are Different from yours are a Challenge:** If you think that you're always right and find yourself getting mad when people disagree, you could be using anger to mask your other emotions. If you see differing opinions as a challenge instead of a varied perspective, you probably need to look closer at your anger.

Reconnecting with Feelings:

If you find yourself getting uncomfortable at the thought of emotions other than anger, or getting stuck in a familiar, harmful response to disruptions in your life, you need to learn how to reconnect with your emotions. The first step is to start noticing your anger triggers and warning signs.

- **The Physical Signs:** Although you probably think that your anger appears out of nowhere with no warning, there are warning signals that show up on a physical level when anger starts. Anger is just one of the many physical responses humans can feel and fuels the fight or flight function in us. The madder you get, the stronger this reaction will be. When you start to notice these signs, you can manage the flow of anger before it takes over.

- **Physical Examples:** Physical signs of anger present in your body include a knotted stomach, clenching your jaw or hands, feeling flushed or clammy, faster breathing, headaches, needing to move or pace, and having difficulty concentrating. You might also tense up your shoulders or have a pounding heart.

Thought Patterns that cause Anger:

You might believe that situations outside of you, such as other people's actions, are what lead to your anger. However, anger issues have more to do with your thoughts about a situation than the actual situation. Here are some negative patterns of thought that can cause you to feel very angry:

- **Overgeneralization**: Overgeneralizing can lead you to feel very angry. For example, saying "Everyone is so disrespectful to me" is a quick way to get mad.

- **Assuming**: Trying to read people's minds or making assumptions can cause you to feel disrespected and thus angry.

- **Having "should" Thoughts**: When you have a rigid idea of how things must go, you will get mad when circumstances don't align with that idea.

- **Blaming Others**: When something doesn't go right, an angry person will always look for someone else to blame. Instead of taking responsibility, you will blame someone else for what has happened to you.

- **Looking for Reasons to be Upset:** Angry people often search for reasons to be upset, blowing things out of proportion or ignoring the positive. Allowing these irritations to build up can cause you to explode over something small.

Who Stresses You Out?

If you struggle with anger, you probably have a few circumstances or people in your life that lead to this emotion. If there is a person who consistently angers you, this could be a signal that you shouldn't spend as much time around them. There will always be people you have to be around with no choice in the matter, such as an irritating boss or co-worker, but in terms of the people you choose to be around, it might be wise to take an inventory of who is causing you stress and spend less time around them.

Remembering to Calm yourself:

As soon as you can recognize the signs that your anger is on the rise, you can handle it fast before it hurts you or those around you. You can start by focusing on how the anger makes you feel physically. Although it sounds counterintuitive, paying attention to these signals can actually lessen the intensity of the frustration at the moment.

Massage yourself:

You can calm yourself down by reaching back to massage your neck and shoulders. Don't forget to breathe deeply, in addition to this, especially by going outside to get some fresh air. Try to get all of your senses engaged with your surroundings, picturing your favorite place, listening to your favorite music, and immersing yourself in your environment.

Reality Checks:

When your anger is threatening to take over, you can bring yourself back to a calmer state by doing reality checks. As soon as you begin to get upset, pause and consider what's happening, asking yourself some of the following questions:

- How much does this matter in the big picture?

- Is this worth feeling horrible over?
- Should I really ruin my day with this?
- Is my reaction reasonable or appropriate?
- How can I change this situation?
- Is it worthwhile to take action and change this?

Once you have decided that what's happening is actually worth your anger, and you can do something to change it, the next step is expressing the anger in a constructive and healthy manner. When you communicate and channel your anger effectively and respectfully, it can be a great inspiration and energy source for changing your life or the issue at hand.

Get Specific about the Feeling:

Another useful way to defuse your anger and work with it in a healthy way is to pinpoint the true feeling behind your anger. Have you been in a fight over something trivial and ridiculous? Huge fights can happen over nothing, such as forgetting to take the trash out, but there is typically something larger happening beneath this.

Walk Away if Needed:

When you find your anger spiraling out of control, take yourself out of the situation so you can cool down. A quick burst of exercise, a walk around the block, meditation, or listening to a song can give you time to cool off, release the emotion, and come back to the problem with a more solution-oriented mindset.

Be Fair in your Fights:

It's fine to get mad at someone. However, without fair fighting, you will see that the relationship breaks down quite fast. Fair fights will let you share what you need while listening to and respecting the other. This is the only way to reach a positive resolution when it comes to interpersonal issues.

Other Healthy Ways to Let Anger out:

If you notice your anger and irritation is on the rise, ask yourself what you're truly getting angry over. Finding out what is causing your frustration will aid you in communicating the feeling in a constructive way and finding a good resolution. You can also follow some of these tips to get your anger under control:

- **Be Present:** As soon as you are caught up in anger's heat, it can be easy to throw out insults or other expressions of frustration, either for yourself or other people. It's also easy to blame others for the way you are or the difficult aspects of your life. Instead of blaming others from the past, think about the present moment from a mindset of finding solutions.

- **Prioritize the Relationship:** Next time you find yourself getting mad in an interpersonal situation, make strengthening and maintaining the relationship more important than being the winner of the argument. This will help you respect the other person. Confrontations and conflicts are tiring, so start thinking about whether your anger is worth this energy. When you fight and argue over every tiny issue, other people are not going to take your concerns seriously.

- **Forgiveness:** Fixing conflicts (either with others or yourself) is impossible without forgiveness. Finding solutions relies on getting rid of the desire to punish other people, which doesn't help. To truly get past your anger problem, you have to learn how to let things go when needed. If you aren't able to agree on something, agree to move past it. When a conflict is just getting worse, sometimes it's best to walk away.

- **Conflict Resolution:** Your pattern for responding to disagreements and differences at work and home can lead to riffs and hostility, or it can lead to trust and safety, depending on how you handle things. Strengthening your conflict resolution skills will lead to better relationships and a lessened anger problem for you.

Finding Professional Help for your Anger:

If you still find that, even after trying all of the tools in this book, your anger is taking over, you may need some more help. Many programs, classes, and therapists exist to help people with anger issues. This can be helpful because you'll connect with others who understand your plight.

- **Practicing new Skills:** Therapy for anger management can help you find out why you feel so angry. Many people have anger but don't know where it's coming from, which makes it nearly impossible to control. Therapy can help you identify your anger triggers in a healthy, safe environment. It will also teach you new skills for expressing it.

- **Groups or Classes:** Groups or classes for anger management let you hear the accounts of other people who are going through the same struggle. This will teach you techniques and tips for managing frustration.

When to Consider Professional Assistance:

If the following apply to you, it's time to think about professional assistance for managing your anger:

- You are always angry or frustrated, even after trying to calm yourself down.

- Your anger leads to a relationship or work problems consistently.

- You've been in legal trouble because of your frustration and anger.

- Your frustration has caused physical altercations.

- If a family member has issues with anger that affect you.

Dealing with a Family Member's Anger:

If it's your relative or other loved one that has an issue with anger, you are probably always afraid of setting them off. But keep in mind that it's not your fault that they are angry. Verbally or physically abusive behavior is never okay. You should be able to expect respect, but when you are being disrespected, you can control the way you handle it and respond. Here are some tips for handling this in a positive way.

- Set personal boundaries so that they know what you are not prepared to tolerate.

- Discuss the problem when you are not fighting instead of when you're both already angry.

- Don't hesitate to remove yourself and walk away if your relative or loved one refuses to get calm.

- Think about therapy or counseling if you can't assert yourself when this person lashes out at you.

- Make sure you are taking your own safety seriously and remove yourself if your safety feels threatened.

The real issue with abusive relationships is not anger. Abuse and domestic violence are actually methods people use to control others, not just an issue of the loss of control. If you're part of a relationship that is abusive, couple's therapy is not the answer. Your partner may need special treatment and counseling, not just classes or group therapy.

CONCLUSION

Thank you for reading *Anger Management: 7 Steps to Freedom from Anger, Stress, and Anxiety*. Hopefully, this book has given you a better understanding of the origins of anger, justified versus unjustified anger, the benefits of this feeling, and the dangers it can present.

If you don't learn to handle your anger in constructive ways now, you will risk serious health problems, difficulties forming and keeping relationships, and trouble in every other area of life. Give yourself the gift of freedom from this emotion and start living the life you were meant to live!

Keep in mind that the more you practice these tactics and methods, the easier it will be to control your anger problem and choose healthier responses to this feeling inside of you. Eventually, you will notice that your anger has less control over your life.

Once again, don't forget to grab a copy of your Free Bonus book *"How to Talk to Anyone: 50 Best Tips and Tricks to Build Instant Rapport"*. If you want to increase your influence and become more effective in your conversations then this book is for you.

Just go to

http://ryanjames.successpublishing.club/freebonus/

Thank you for reading and good luck on your path to emotional wellness.

THANK YOU!

Before you go, I just wanted to say thank you for purchasing my book.

You could have picked from dozens of other books on the same topic but you took a chance and chose this one.

So, a HUGE thanks to you for getting this book and for reading all the way to the end.

Now I wanted to ask you for a small favor. **Could you please take just a few minutes to leave a review for this book on Amazon?**

This feedback will help me continue to write the type of books that will help you get the results you want. So if you enjoyed it, please let me know! (-:

www.ingramcontent.com/pod-product-compliance
Lightning Source LLC
Chambersburg PA
CBHW071724020426
42333CB00017B/2383